The Hand of Yahweh
Upon The Holy Spirit

By:

Prophet Anthony Montoya

The Hand Of Yahweh Upon The Holy Spirit

By

Prophet Anthony Montoya

Copyright @ 2018, All Rights Reserved
Printed in The United States of America

Published By:

ABM Publications
A division of Andrew Bills Ministries Inc.
PO Box 6811, Orange, CA 92863

ISBN: 978-1-931820-88-2

DEDICATION

Special thanks to My Mother and Father,

Santiago and Mary,

To my daughter, Alexis Marina Montoya,

And to Lily Avila and Mr. Burns

PROPHET ANTHONY MONTOYA

TABLE OF CONTENTS

PROPHET ANTHONY MONTOYA

Chapter 1

The hand of Yah 2/17/2016, this revelation was given to me after 21 days of consecration. **Judges 16:22 Howbeit the hair of his head began to grow again after he was shaven. This interpretation of Gods glory resides within us. Samson's hair began to grow after it was shaven. Ephesians 3:20 Now to Him who is able to [carry out His purpose and] do superabundantly more than all that we dare ask or think [infinitely beyond our greatest prayers, hopes, or dreams], according to His power that is at work within us.** There is such a divine grace and mercy that has increased within the spirit realm as he leads us into his divine glory that's attached to us.

In the book of Isaiah 65:24 24 "It shall also come to pass that before they call, I will answer; and while they are still speaking, I will hear. The father says I will answer them before they even call to me. While they are still thinking about their needs, I will go ahead and answer their prayers. There is such a grace of himself that resides with you the third DNA strand of his chromosomes from your father from heaven which is Spiritual Timing! The body of Christ needs to understand spiritual timing in all things of the spiritual gifts and natural.

1John 2:6 He that saith he abideth in him ought himself also walk, even as he walked. [6] whoever says he lives in Christ [that is, whoever says he has accepted Him as God and Savior] ought [as a moral obligation] to walk *and* conduct himself just as He walked *and* conducted Himself. There is a level of transition of character and metamorphosis that has been released within us, even as

he thinketh his desires, it is given to you, before you even pray about it. This means your thoughts have been lifted up as prayers. Adam was lonely and he received a wife. There was a petition in his heart for something that already was, and it was given to him before he prayed for or a chance to pray for it.

This level of transition has graduated unto you this day even when you're talking to someone, or even when you think about someone being made whole it shall happen. Your thoughts shall be understood, when you're thinking God has collected it from you even as a prayer and it shall be established as a prayer. Dimension of Epekiazo, the glory cloud that resides within you only when you desire for his divine character. You are altering into a state of transition in your life most of the things that are given to you have not prayed for it.

When you think about someone and you want them to be blessed, doors are opening for them all of a sudden so God gets all the glory! **Joshua 24:13 And I have given you a land for which ye did not labor (a place of Intercession or toil prayer), and cities which ye built not, and ye dwell in them; of the vineyards and olive yards which ye planted not do ye eat.**

Jeremiah 1:5, "Before I formed you in the womb I knew you, before you were born I set you apart; I appointed you as a prophet to the nations." Now saints more revelation. Before I formed thee in the belly I knew thee (You and We were with him in him and heaven the bosom of his chromosomes) before thou camest forth out of the womb I sanctified thee, and I ordained thee a Prophet unto the nations. Now a revelation of correction (God and Seer).

This meaning is Past, Present, and Future. Created by a different chromosome! **Isaiah 55:11 So will My word be which goes out of My mouth; It will not return to Me void (useless, without result),Without accomplishing what I desire, And without succeeding *in the matter* for which I sent it. It shall prosper in the thing where I sent it.**

1 Peter 1:23 [22] **Since by your obedience to the truth you have purified yourselves for a sincere love of the believers, [see that you] love one another from the heart [always unselfishly seeking the best for one another],** [23] **for you have been born again [that is, reborn from above—spiritually transformed, renewed, and set apart for His purpose] not of seed which is perishable but [from that which is] imperishable *and* immortal, *that is,* through the living and everlasting word of God.** Reborn not from a mortal origin (Seed, Sperm) but from one that is immortal by the everlasting word of God Yah!

1 John 3: [8] **the one who practices sin [separating himself from God, and offending Him by acts of disobedience, indifference, or rebellion] is of the devil [and takes his inner character and moral values from him, not God]; for the devil has sinned *and* violated God's law from the beginning. The Son of God appeared for this purpose, to destroy the works of the devil.** [9] **No one who is born of God [deliberately, knowingly, and habitually] practices sin, because** [a]**God's seed [His principle of life, the essence of His righteous character] remains [permanently] in him [who is born again—who is reborn from above—spiritually transformed, renewed, and set apart for His purpose]; and he [who is born again] cannot *habitually* [live a life characterized by] sin, because he is born of God *and* longs to please Him.** [10] **By this the**

children of God and the children of the devil are clearly identified: anyone who does not practice righteousness [who does not seek God's will in thought, action, and purpose] is not of God, nor is the one who does not [unselfishly] [b]love his [believing] brother.
[11] For this is the message which you [believers] have heard from the beginning [of your relationship with Christ], that we should [unselfishly] love *and* seek the best for one another; [12] and not be like Cain, who was of the evil one and murdered his brother [Abel]. And why did he murder him? Because Cain's deeds were evil, and his brothers were righteous.

Seeking the best for one another in thought and action, meaning giving, aiding, help promoting one another in their ministry for Gods kingdom and not selfish intention of our own. God made manifest his son and came to this world for full redemption to destroy, loosen, dissolve the laws the devil has done.

Let's recap this one more time: [9] No one who is born of God [deliberately, knowingly, and habitually] practices sin, because [a]God's seed [His principle of life, the essence of His righteous character] remains [permanently] in him [who is born again—who is reborn from above—spiritually transformed, renewed, and set apart for His purpose]; and he [who is born again] cannot *habitually* [live a life characterized by] sin, because he is born of God *and* longs to please Him.

The sperm of his divine character is what we, are whole being should desire! Everyone has been preached the word of God and the Seed is Christ, so all blessing comes along with it yes. Yes but his revelation is us yearning for his

Divine Character! He is speaking of his Divine character that never dies or fades away or (Rot tens) Immortality. How is it precious rocks, lives and don't decay for millions of millions of years, rubies, gems, form over time.

Proverbs 31:10 a wife of noble character who can find? She is worth far more than rubies" we are more precious than gemstones. How do ye receive this dimension of his glory it's his Character impartation.

This basis of scripture should saturate our whole being. **2 Peter 3:9 [9] The Lord does not delay [as though He were unable to act] and is not slow about His promise, as some count slowness, but is [extraordinarily] patient toward you, not wishing for any to perish but for all to come to repentance.** The blood of repentance over our lives, every time we pray before the courts of heaven, summoning our accuser and agreeing with him and pleading the blood of Repentance over our lives.

Exodus 7:1 7 Then the Lord said to Moses, "Now hear this: I make you as God to Pharaoh [to declare my will and purpose to him]; and your brother Aaron shall be your prophet. There is only a few select that have been chosen will rightfully come into this transition into immortality the fivefold ministry Sons of God! You notice the scripture says I make you as god to Pharaoh. A god over him not a Prophet!

John 10:34 Yeshua answered them, "Is it not written in your law" I have said you are gods! This is what Yeshua was crucified for calling himself God and speaking the forbidden name Yahushua, Eyeh Asher Eyeh the name of his Father. He said he was God! They are distinctly one, its

ok to call yourself God or a God cause your one with him!
You're not implying that you are thee God but one with
Him a God! Miracles can only be performed by Gods.
Creative miracles.

If you do not catch this vision you will die like mere men.
Our next transition is not Titles of the law of men, but Sons
of God, Gods. **Romans 8:19 for the creation waits with
eager longing for the revealing of the sons of God.** Even if
you're not called by God, a man chosen or loyal to God, a
God a son can call you into Ministry to change the life and
destiny of purpose in your life! I have given you Power to
give life and Take life! If ye cannot receive this, you cannot
be considered a God! Did not Moses send forth Plagues to
destroy and take life? Did not he call out every first born of
Egypt Shall Die!

**Judges 13:5 [5] for behold, you shall conceive and give birth
to a son. No razor shall come upon his head, for the boy
shall be a [b] Nazirite [dedicated] to God from birth; and
he shall begin to rescue Israel from the hands of the
Philistines."** His mission as the born child was to initiate
the deliverance process not finish it. This was a fore
shadow of Yeshua in the future dying on the cross to finish
the Deliverance process the completion. You can be so
close to someone but far from their source, and also never
of influence, never tapped into what they have or been
with your grace even for a moment. That is why some or
many have run from you or walked away from you. Your
source of energy is hidden from them and you have much
back up from heaven, but they see you as ordinary folk.

The same certificate of authority to raise the dead and heal
the sick is the same certificated of sending or releasing

someone away or from your presence as dismissing them. People need to know you can kill or destroy. Yeshua took the keys of life and death. **Isaiah 22:22 I will place on his shoulder the key to the house of David, what he opens no one can shut, and what he shuts no man can open. The power and authority of life and death, curse or blessing, prosperity and plague. Isaiah 45: [7] I form the light and create darkness, I make peace [national well-being] and I create [physical] [a]evil (calamity); I am the Lord, Who does all these things.**

Yes, it does state in his word to pray and bless those that persecute you and talk all manner of evil against you. There is point where enough is enough! People need to know you can send curse and plagues their way because you are a God! No longer a prophet or apostle! If society took away law enforcement they, rebellion would run ramped. This is a key antidote to govern righteousness here on earth.

Deuteronomy 34:12 and for all the mighty power and all the great deeds of terror that Moses did in the sight of all Israel. This is only for leadership, it's not about that we can kill and send plagues and terror but we can!

Chapter 2

Acts 13 [8] But Elymas [a]the wise man—for that is the translation of his name [[b]which he had given himself]—opposed them, seeking to keep the proconsul from accepting the faith. People who are talking about you and trying to cause division and discord or even your destiny, purpose everything that is rightfully yours to by his kingdom commission, by spiritual timing.
[9] But Saul, who is also called Paul, filled with *and* controlled by the Holy Spirit, looked steadily at [Elymas] [10] And said, You master in every form of deception *and* recklessness, unscrupulousness, *and* wickedness, you son of the devil, you enemy of everything that is upright *and* good, will you never stop perverting *and* making crooked the straight paths of the Lord *and* plotting against His saving purposes?
[11] And now, behold, the hand of the Lord is upon you, and you will be blind, [so blind that you will be] unable to see the sun for a time. Instantly there fell upon him a mist and a darkness, and he groped about seeking persons who would lead him by the hand.

Suddenly a disaster was sent to blind him for disrupting your ministry. So just because you are wise and have understanding, but you were not called by God or me, meaning if your called by man in ministry without the approval of heaven or mans wicked intent you are in trouble. You can maneuver in ministry with gift out of the absence of God's presence and divine character and without the leading and timing of Holy Spirit.

Doesn't the scripture state, God lord did I not prophesy in your name, heal the sick, then God says, you worker of iniquity I never knew you.

The father says the gift is not me and I am not the gift. Get this revelation. **1 Samuel 6: [7] "Now then, make a new cart and prepare two [b]milk cows on which a yoke has never been placed; and hitch the cows to the cart and take their calves back home, away from them. [8] "Then take the ark of the Lord and put it on the cart; and put the articles of gold which you are returning to Him as a guilt offering in a box beside it. Then send it away [without a driver].**

They used flesh cattle to carry the Ark of the Covenant from the philistines. The more anointing comes flesh, flesh carries the anointing, God is not the anointing, anointing adds more flesh to flesh. God is not flesh, even though his son came to earth made of flesh born of a man. When you're more anointed, you can become more carnal, you need to sacrifice your flesh more when anointing hits you more.

When the anointing comes more, flesh needs to be sacrificed. You become so spiritual and no earthly good. **Matthew 16:18 And I say to you that you are [d]Peter, and on this [e]rock I will build My church; and the [f]gates of Hades (death) will not overpower it [by preventing the resurrection of the Christ]. [19] I will give you the keys (authority) of the kingdom of heaven; and whatever you bind [forbid, declare to be improper and unlawful] on earth [g]will have [already] been bound in heaven, and whatever you lose [permit, declare lawful] on earth [h]will have [already] been loosed in heaven." [20] Then He gave the disciples strict orders to tell no one that He was the**

Christ (the Messiah, the Anointed). Every spiritual law created by the devil is legislation. Gates are considered tools. **Judges 16:3 [3] But Samson lay until midnight, and [then] he arose and took hold of the doors of the city's gate and the two posts, and pulling them up, bar and all, he put them on his shoulders and carried them to the top of the hill that is before Hebron.**

Saints you notice in verse 4 after he took up the gates his direction was altered different, **Verse 4: After this he loved a woman in the Valley of Sorek whose name was Delilah.**

The gates you carry can cause purpose and destiny in people lives you can open or shut cause life or destruction.

Chapter 3

Let me give you some more revelation, a man Adam was born from the dust of the Earth. A woman was created from an unfinished product, she became a finished product, and she was created from a life created organism not man. A woman is a product of life that causes happiness. When you receive more anointing and when you pray, pray for the adequate submission of accuracy. This is what I mean, it's not all about the receiving but to be subjected unto sacrifice of the flesh, first is the subjecting of sacrifice then the receiving.

There is an adequate sacrificial subjection of sacrifice that was already paid and can receive it. Not my will be done but thy will be done Father! Many have received but also missed the mark the timing and filled with Pride. Sometimes you will fast and pray and receive but possible die spiritually out of character through compromise. Yeshua prayed for the spiritual sacrificial subjection first!

You must demand from the father take all my emotions and feelings from me be in control of them. **Psalms 131: My soul is quieted liked a weaned child. Now saints let's move on to the Revelation of Wells and Suffice Interpretation of Increase!**

John 1: [38] But Jesus turned, and as He saw them following Him, He said to them, what are you looking for? [And what is it you wish?] And they answered Him, Rabbi— which translated is Teacher—where are you staying? [39] He said to them, Come and see. So they went and saw where He was staying, and they remained with Him [k]

that day. It was then about the tenth hour (about four o'clock in the afternoon). Yahushua took them to a place where Yeshua had Title deed to a place of land and his own Property! Yahushua was walking in Increase and Favor!

Isaiah 12:23 ² Behold, God, my salvation! I will trust and not be afraid, for the Lord God is my strength and song; yes, He has become my salvation.
³ Therefore with joy will you draw water from the wells of salvation. Salvation does not dwell with just one well, but wells. Preachers for 100 years have preached one well one salvation. There are wells of salvation of forgiveness of sins, wells of acceptance or going to heaven, wells of salvation of your pocket of finances. Wells of salvation of your Health. Wells of salvation of your relationships.

You have been drinking only from one well, your whole lives, salvation and you get to go to heaven, that's not the perfected work, only one well no! The prayer of Yahushua Our father in heaven, Hollowed be thy name thy kingdom come, on earth as it is in Heaven! Everything the kingdom has it shall be established in your life!

You're coming into a place where your finances are born again! The car you drive or don't have, your house, vineyards, wells, houses etc. **1 John 5:4 4 for whatever is born of God is victorious over the world; and this is the victory that conquers the world, even our faith.**

This Revelation of all your belonging have now just been born of God, everything that is attached to you shall conquer and overcome the world system in your life. Material things can be born of God! Here is the reason why we cannot access this water or wells. **Psalms 68:11[9] You, O God, did send a plentiful rain; you did restore *and* confirm your heritage when it languished *and* was weary. [10] Your flock found a dwelling place in it; You, O God, in your goodness did provide for the poor *and* needy. [11] The Lord gives the word [of power]; the women who bear *and* publish [the news] are a great host.**

[12] The kings of the enemies' armies, they flee, they flee! She who tarries at home divides the spoil [left behind].

Jesus Christ return Yahushua Hamashiack is not sufficient! That was not the finished work! Yeshua gave the word and Great was the company that published it! Published it meant to be pronounced and preached and let be known as news! The church who have Marketed Yeshua so great was the company of them that believed and Published to you all one Salvation, only one well his return! That was not the whole Part or Revelation that was provided. They have been spewing out the wrong interpretation! Ignorant was the company that published it. We were never given access to it because we as the company the church published one well.

The Body of Christ has Published to you His Christ return, salvation of going to heaven, manipulating you telling you pay your tithes, and continue to go to church and be under a controlling minister or church or leader for the time is near. Spewing out fear tactics to keep you in control of your lives and destiny and purpose! The problem is that the body of Christ Apostles, prophets, evangelists, pastors and teachers have followed the written word by Greek mindset and doctrine and the compromise of the immature majority of ignorant people that published it,

21

they preached it you believed it! In apostolic ministry leaders have drank demonic potions of compromise and influential drinks as well as poisoned food, by the published majority of ignorance. When your Territory has increased the anointing and their success has so overwhelmed them they have lost the focus of vision of the Leading of the Holy Spirit and his Timing!

Judges 16: 25it so happened when they were in high spirits, that they said, "Call for Samson, that he may amuse us." So they called for Samson from the prison, and he entertained them. And they made him stand between the pillars. 26Then Samson said to the boy who was holding his hand, "Let me feel the pillars on which the house rests, that I may lean against them."

When Samson a great man of God was influenced by a woman and lost or got off track, he was abused and controlled by the published majority and was led to some pillars by a little boy (Meaning compromising with the Majority and Immature) leaders in minister without, the Leading of the holy spirit and Holy spirit's Timing! You can get so caught up in your success your vision is lost or deluded greatly! You begin to only worship your gift and calling and commission and lose sight of Worshipping Yah father son and Holy Spirit!

We are whole lives were going to our neighbor the church or the body asking for money, to receive from a responsible position but only was granted one access of a well salvation and going to heaven. That was the only well that was published to us. You were not all responsible for this! The written word of God was given to us and everything else was provided for but they did not give everything to us all at once. Their interpretation of miscalculating Timing of the Spirit and A racing spirit of gatherings, telling you, you need to come to this teaching, receive this impartation, this class of prophetic teaching etc. for years but no transformation of Dominion!   All this Revelation has finally been Revealed and Leashed out and the Books are open to only the Mature Sons of God! Not just the ones who carry gifts and have large ministries, the ignorant majority crowd! They have not proven to be responsible even until this day. We have been sitting and begging for bread, bleeding for it, a leader preaching the word or doctrine not in a Kingdom fashion of revelation. Give us this day our daily bread! It was already provided for you, we are blessed with all things! You were only given one Salvation of a well the Promise of Going to Heaven!

Malachi1:[6] "'A son honors his father, and a servant his master. Then if I am a Father, where is my honor? And if I am a Master, where is the [reverent] fear *and* respect due me?' says the Lord of hosts to you, O priests, who despise my name. But you say, 'How *and* in what way have we despised your name?' [7] You are presenting defiled food upon my altar. But you say, 'How have we defiled you?' By thinking that the table of the Lord is contemptible *and* may be despised.

There are teaching dog poisoned food and Gods altars, given maggot food as bread! Offering soulish teaching, unforbidden knowledge that you never or had access to by Holy Spirit. Preaching a doctrine of lies, defiled meat. **Verse 8 when you [priests] present the [c]blind [animals] for sacrifice, is it not evil? And when you present the lame and the sick, is it not evil? Offer such a thing [as a blind or lame or sick animal] to your governor [as a gift or as**

payment for your taxes].
Would he be pleased with you? Or would he receive you graciously?" says the Lord of hosts. What is also this information or Revelation my children are in agony, physically tormented, no revelation of understanding in them, no transformation of character and also there not walking in the abundance of wealth which you profess to speak of! There continually before me some 30-fold, 60-fold, half-hearted on my altar!

Malachi 1:[9] "But now will you not entreat God's favor, that He may be gracious to us? With such an offering from your hand [as an imperfect animal for sacrifice], will He show favor to any of you?" says the Lord of hosts. [10] "Oh, that there were even one among you [whose duty it is to minister to me] who would shut the gates, so that you would not kindle *fire on* my altar uselessly [with an empty, worthless pretense]! I am not pleased with you," says the Lord of hosts, "nor will I accept an offering from your hand. [11] For [d]from the rising of the sun, even to its setting, my name shall be great among the nations. In every place incense is going to be offered to my name, and a grain offering that is pure; for my name shall be great among the nations," says the Lord of hosts. Oh that one of you would shut the temple doors, so that you would not light useless fires on my altar. Useless fires on his altar, Partial mixed twisted unforbidden mixture, knowledge teaching lies, abominable speech.

Chapter 4

James 3: [6] and the tongue is a fire. [The tongue is a] world of wickedness set among our members, contaminating *and* depraving the whole body and setting on fire the wheel of birth (the cycle of man's nature), being itself ignited by hell (Gehenna). A word of unrighteousness, the tongue is set among our members, the body offering, staining the whole body, setting on fire the whole course of life, physical, spiritual and economically, set on fire by hell. **Isaiah 50:11 [1] Behold, all you [enemies of your own selves] who attempt to kindle your own fires [and work out your own plans of salvation], who surround *and* gird yourselves with momentary sparks, darts, *and* firebrands that you set aflame!—walk by the light of your self-made fire and of the sparks that you have kindled [for yourself, if you will]! But this shall you have from my hand: you shall lie down in grief *and* in torment.** So, technically we have been given our own torches of sparks and plans of salvation the way we been taught, but was not our own fault, but if you continue this course your own way all you shall receive wells of grief and torment for Gods Right hand! So technically whoever your sitting under you receive also their curse and torment from your leader!

Jude 1:23 (CSB) save others by snatching [them] from the fire; on others have mercy in fear, hating even the garment defiled by the flesh. When others try to aid you in understanding of not going to certain churches or be attached to ungodly soul ties and friends or Christian brothers and sisters you been attached to. You don't listen to correct council you call it judging or gossiping. But many of you have been informed to leave or run from your course of life and ignored the warnings! That means even the money or churched you're involved with and the offering you drop in the basket opens demonic doors to your lifestyle! It specifically stated even your own garments are defiled by flesh, meaning your material things are cursed and are not born again!

It is your ignorance of who you follow! **Malachi 1:[12] "But you [priests] profane it when you say, 'The table of the Lord is defiled, and as for its fruit, its food is to be despised.' [13] You also say, 'How tiresome this is!' And you disdainfully sniff at it," says the Lord of hosts, "and you bring what was taken by robbery, and the lame or the sick [animals]; this you bring as an offering! Should I receive it with pleasure from your hand?" says the Lord. [14] "But cursed is the swindler who has a male in his flock and vows [to offer] it, but sacrifices to the Lord a blemished _or_ diseased thing! For I am a great King," says the Lord of hosts, "and my name is to be [reverently and greatly] feared among the nations."**

This meaning an imperfection that man or impair a flaw or something out of alignment. Now a blemish is something thought to mar the appearance or character of a thing. The motive and intentions of the Heart! The desirable thing that is different to see or very difficult to discern!

Malachi 2 "Now, O priests, this commandment is for you. [2] If you do not listen, and if you do not take it to heart to honor My name," says the Lord of hosts, "then I will send the curse upon you and I will curse your blessings [on the people]. Indeed, I have cursed them already, because you are not taking it to heart. [3] Behold, I am going to rebuke your seed, and I will spread the refuse on your faces, the

refuse from the festival offerings; and you will be taken away with it [in disgrace]. ⁴ Then you will know [without any doubt] that I have sent this [new] commandment to you (priests), that My covenant may continue with Levi [the priestly tribe]," says the Lord of hosts. ⁵ "My covenant with Levi was [one of] life and peace, and I gave them to him as an object of reverence; so he [and the priests] feared Me and stood in reverent awe of My name. ⁶ True instruction was in Levi's mouth and injustice was not found on his lips. He walked with me in peace and uprightness, and he turned many from wickedness.

It states I will curse your blessings on the people hello. ⁶ True instruction was in Levi's mouth and injustice was not found on his lips. He walked with me in peace and uprightness, and he turned many from wickedness. ⁷ For the lips of the priest should guard *and* preserve knowledge [of my law], and the people should seek instruction from his mouth; for he is the messenger of the Lord of hosts. ⁸ But as for you [priests], you have turned from the way and you have caused many to stumble by your instruction [in the law]. You have violated the covenant of Levi," says the Lord of hosts. False teaching was on your lips the leaders.

They have defiled God not by Tithes and offering but by their words, verse 17 you have wearied the Lord with your words. But you say, "In what way have we wearied Him?" In that you say, "Everyone who does evil is good in the sight of the Lord, and He delights in them," or [by asking], "Where is the God of justice?" The incorrect interpretation of the scripture and not revelation of the correct interpretation! Meaning the preachers and leaders, what are they saying when they interpret the scriptures with a

Greek mindset and Latin mindset or out of a twisted intention or motive of the heart!   When Adam sinned, the sacrificial offering had to be made. The sacrifice of sin had to be atoned for. In the book of Genesis, God went into the forest and sacrificed an animal for their sins.

Genesis 3:[21] For Adam also and for his wife the Lord God made long coats (tunics) of skins and clothed them. [22] And the Lord God said, Behold, the man has become like one of Us [the Father, Son, and Holy Spirit], to know [how to distinguish between] good and evil *and* blessing and calamity; and now, lest he put forth his hand and take also from the tree of life and eat, and live [b]forever—. They had to be clothed with Salvation!

The forgiveness of their sins! The tree of life is Christ! He had to cover not only the soul and spirit of Adam and eve but also thy physical body of Adam and eve. Salvation of their soul, spirit and the physical part of man, (Material)!

Exodus 12: [21] Then Moses called for all the elders of Israel and said to them, "Go and take a lamb for yourselves according to [the size of] your families and slaughter the Passover *lamb*. [22] You shall take a bunch of [e]hyssop, dip it in the blood which is in the basin, and touch some of the blood to the lintel [above the doorway] and to the two doorposts; and none of you shall go outside the door of his house until morning.

A Memorial of Redemption

[23] For the Lord will pass through to strike the Egyptians; and when He sees the blood on the lintel [above the entry way] and on the two doorposts, the Lord will pass

over the door and will not allow [f]the destroyer to come into your houses to slay you. [24] You shall observe this event [concerning Passover] as an ordinance for you and for your children forever. [25] When you enter the land which the Lord will give you, as He has promised, you shall keep *and* observe this service.

The lamb which was already sacrificed for you and me, when you die to self, your financial state has to change. Verse [35] Now the Israelites had acted in accordance with the word of Moses; and they had asked the Egyptians for articles of silver and articles of gold, and clothing. [36] The Lord gave the people favor in the sight of the Egyptians, so that they gave them what they asked. And so they plundered the Egyptians [of those things].

They plundered the Egyptians of their material wealth, silver and gold! Stripped them bare naked! Passover is the month of March and April the day he delivered us from Egypt and all its demonic dominion it had over us! That means diseases, health, relationships, material, strongholds etc.

Exodus 11:2 Then the Lord said to Moses, "I will bring yet one more plague on Pharaoh and on Egypt; after that he will let you go. When he lets you go, he will most certainly drive you out of here completely. [2] speak so that all of the people [of Israel] may hear, and tell every man to ask from his neighbor, and every woman to ask from her neighbor, articles of silver, and articles of gold." [3] The Lord gave the people favor in the sight of the Egyptians. Moreover, the man Moses was greatly esteemed in the land of Egypt, [both] in the sight of Pharaoh's servants and in the sight of the people.

The body of Christ is ordered to receive from a responsible leader to receive silver, gold and title deeds to land! Moses did not keep all this wealth to himself but gave to all of them!

It is a very serious thing of the father for you to have your own piece of land, houses you have not built, wells you did not dig and vineyards you did not plant he shall supply thee! Saints well I was writing this Revelation, the father told me that, his children that was receiving this teaching where I minister, Ray glory ministries they have graduated to this state of Transition. Here are some testimonies which accured when I was given the revelation. Not going to mention names, but one Prophetess mother prayed and told God let my son become so sick, that he does not want to do drugs again. The report was overheard that her son was really sick for two days even he was off the drugs.

Now she did not speak life or blessing but sent a small plague to stop him in his tracks. The next prayer she prayed for her son that was still messing up, she told God let him come to the end of his road and hit a brick wall so his eyes will open!

Within a few days he hit a wall and broke his right toe and was in a cast walking around 2/2016. One of her granddaughters who is a senior in high school who sits under these teachings for quite some time, she was at the mall and bought something to eat, and all the tables were full. She asked the father please can I have just one table to sit down and eat, within seconds the mall alarms went off and every food table was cleared, and the father told her pick a table. He gave her the whole floor to choose from! One husband and wife, that sits under these teachings also, the wife in management, a certain manager was scheduling and typing emails and making up false instructions and leadings without her approval and didn't know what was going on. So, the wife, found out about all this misleading lies behind her back, she told the father he needs to be removed, this was her prayer! Within 2 weeks that person was on a ski trip and broke one leg and three ribs and is no longer there!

PROPHET ANTHONY MONTOYA

Chapter 5

Let's move on saints, to revelation of his word. **Genesis 1:2 2 the earth was without form and an empty waste, and darkness was upon the face of the very great deep.**
The Spirit of God was moving (hovering, brooding) over the face of the waters. Brooding in Hebrew means Rachaph (Fertilizing, to shake or move). A **fertilizer** or **fertiliser** (in British English) is any material of natural or synthetic origin (other than liming materials) that is applied to soils or to plant tissues (usually leaves) to supply one or more plant nutrients essential to the growth of plants. The Spirit of Yah Holy Spirit!

Fertilizers enhance the growth of plants. This goal is met in (two ways), the traditional one being additives that provide nutrients. The second mode by which some fertilisers act is to enhance the effectiveness of the soil by modifying its (water retention and aeration). This article, like most on fertilizers, emphasizes the nutritional aspect. Fertilizers typically provide, in varying proportions: [1]

- three main macronutrients:
    - Nitrogen (N): leaf growth;
    - Phosphorus (P): Development of roots, flowers, seeds, fruit;
    - Potassium (K): Strong stem growth, movement of water in plants, promotion of flowering and fruiting;
- three secondary macronutrients: calcium (Ca), magnesium (Mg), and Sulphur (S);

- micronutrients: copper (Cu), iron (Fe), manganese (Mn), molybdenum (Mo), zinc (Zn), boron (B), and of occasional significance there are silicon (Si), cobalt (Co), and vanadium (V) plus rare mineral catalysts.

Incubating 2. (to hatch (eggs), as by sitting upon them or by artificial (heat). 3. To maintain at a favorable temperature and in other conditions promoting development, as cultures of bacteria or prematurely born infants. Now you notice there is three mechanisms that are in this process! This first mode is one being additives that provide nutrients. The second mode is to enhance the effectiveness of the soil by modifying (convert, change or transform), its water retention and aeration. Water retention the flow (**Water retention**, also known as fluid retention refers to an excessive buildup of fluid in the circulatory system, body tissues, or cavities in the body.

Aeration (also called **aerification**) is the process by which air is circulated through, mixed with or dissolved in a liquid or substance. Also this had to do with the flow!

Now you know there are three mechanisms that are described here but one being hidden which is the Heat! Now you know earth produces Heat and cold temperatures which relate to at different timings!

Ecclesiastes 3 speaks of timing for everything! **Jeremiah 1:5 before I formed thee in the belly I knew thee; and before thou camest forth out of the womb I sanctified thee, *and* I ordained thee a prophet unto the nations.** First I knew thee, second I sanctified thee (Purpose and destiny) ordained is to be set up part!

Matthew 3:11 "I baptize you with water for repentance. But after me comes one who is more powerful than I, whose sandals I am not worthy to carry. He will baptize you with the Holy Spirit and fire. Water, Heat needs to be under subjection of the Holy spirits timing and order!

The father is speaking of Order and Timing of the orchestrasration of the Holy Spirit and Demonstration of its power! that is totally different from Gift! God is not the Gift and the Gift is not God!

Isaiah 10:27 so it will be in that day, that the burden of the Assyrian will be removed from your shoulders and his yoke from your neck. The yoke will be broken because of the fat. Fat in Hebrew means cheleb, the rich choice part the Marrow! The marrow has to do with the Bones! Some bibles say the Anointing. The Holy Spirit breaks the yoke! The Anointing is oil which is understanding. Holy Spirit releases the affirming of anointing for closure, affirmation, clarity, understanding, confirmation etc. The Holy Spirit reveals to you the root cause of what's going on.

We all know the gift, can be what watered down, and watered-down teaching, false impregnation, prophecies that are watered down! You would want the full Demonstration of the Authority which is the Holy Spirit order and the Dominion of the full Demonstration of Holy spirits power! Which all has to do with Spiritual Timing! You all know you can prophesy and use the gifts out of the absence of the presence of the Father!

When you pray ask for the adequate subjection of sacrifice of the flesh! When Yeshua prayed and said let not my will be done but yours! He was clothed inwardly and outwardly of Glory! But he needed his own earthly flesh to be under subjection of the will of the father and his Timing! Also pray for impartation of spiritual timing! Pray for the impartation of his divine character! Dying to yourself and self-will!

Genesis 2:[9] And out of the ground the Lord God made to grow every tree that is pleasant to the sight *or* to be desired—good (suitable, pleasant) for food; the tree of life also in the center of the garden, and the tree of the knowledge of [the difference between] good and evil *and* blessing and calamity. The tree of life was Christ! The second tree was the tree of knowledge and power!

Ezekiel 28:[12] Son of man, take up a lamentation over the king of Tyre and say to him, thus says the Lord God: You are the full measure *and* pattern of exactness [giving the finishing touch to all that constitutes completeness], full of wisdom and perfect in beauty. [13] You were in [a] Eden, the garden of God; every precious stone was your covering, the carnelian, topaz, jasper, chrysolite, beryl, onyx, sapphire, carbuncle, and emerald; and your settings and your sockets *and* engravings were wrought in gold. On the day that you were created they were prepared. [14] You were the anointed cherub that covers with overshadowing [wings], and I set you so. You were upon the holy mountain of God; you walked up and down in the midst of the stones of fire [like the paved work of gleaming sapphire stone upon which the God of Israel walked on Mount Sinai].

[15] You were blameless in your ways from the day you were created until iniquity *and* guilt were found in you.

[16] Through the abundance of your commerce (Economic trade riches or treasures) you were filled with lawlessness *and* violence, and you sinned; therefore, I cast you out as a profane

thing from the mountain of God and the guardian cherub drove you out from the midst of the stones of fire.

[17] Your heart was proud *and* lifted up because of your beauty; you corrupted your wisdom for the sake of your splendor. I cast you to the ground; I lay you before kings that they might gaze at you.

[18] You have profaned your sanctuaries by the multitude of your iniquities *and* the enormity of your guilt, by the unrighteousness of your trade. Therefore, I have brought forth a fire from your midst; it has consumed you, and I have reduced you to ashes upon the earth in the sight of all who looked at you.

Satan wanted to become greater to than the most-high, he ate of the tree of knowledge and power he wanted to increase his territory! Disobedience is considered Treason!

Let's recap **Ezekiel 28: verse 3 and 4** [with] **your own wisdom and with your own understanding you have gotten you riches *and* power and have brought gold and silver into your treasuries;**

[5] **By your great wisdom and by your traffic you have increased your riches *and* power, and your heart is proud *and* lifted up because of your wealth;**

Trafficking is commerce, trade, human trafficking forced labor or sexual exploitation! Satan committed treason and also tricked 1/3 of the angels traded with them something! He committed spiritual adultery! Which then came to what? **Genesis 6: 6 when men began to multiply on the face of the land and daughters were born to them,**

[2] **The sons of God saw that the daughters of men were fair, and they took wives of all they desired *and* chose.**

[3] Then the Lord said, My Spirit shall not forever dwell *and* strive with man, for he also is flesh; but his days shall yet be 120 years.

[4] There were giants on the earth in those days—and also afterward—when the sons of God lived with the daughters of men, and they bore children to them. These were the mighty men who were of old, men of renown.

Genesis 2: [16] And the Lord God commanded the man, saying, you may freely eat of every tree of the garden;

[17] But of the tree of the knowledge of good and evil *and* blessing and calamity you shall not eat, for in the day that you eat of it you shall surely die. This was an act of Obedience and trust! He never said don't ever eat of it! There is a timing when he would allow them to eat of it! God is a father of Knowledge and Power!

Genesis 2: [21] And the Lord God caused a deep sleep to fall upon Adam; and while he slept, He took one of his ribs *or* a part of his side and closed up the [place with] flesh.

[22] And the rib *or* part of his side which the Lord God had taken from the man He built up *and* made into a woman, and He brought her to the man.

The father created woman out of a rib, man was created from dust! Woman was created out of the bone marrow finished product! The blood is manufactured within the bones, Yeshua's bones were crushed!

Genesis 3: 3 now the serpent was more subtle *and* crafty than any living creature of the field which the Lord God had made. And he [Satan] said to the woman, Can it really be that God has said, you shall not eat from every tree of the garden?

² And the woman said to the serpent, we may eat the fruit from the trees of the garden,

³ Except the fruit from the tree which is in the middle of the garden. God has said, you shall not eat of it, neither shall you touch it, lest you die.

⁴ But the serpent said to the woman, you shall not surely die,

⁵ For God knows that in the day you eat of it your eyes will be opened, and you will be like God, knowing the difference between good and evil *and* blessing and calamity.

⁶ And when the woman saw that the tree was good (suitable, pleasant) for food and that it was delightful to look at, and a tree to be desired in order to make one wise, she took of its fruit and ate; and she gave some also to her husband, and he ate.

Now what entered eve first, the spirit of Reason before she ate of the apple! Lots daughters said let's get our father drunk because there's no men on this earth, so we can bear children! Which is reasoning! Sarah gave her husband her maid because she said she was too old! This is called reasoning, we received the curse of our Father Abraham and Adam! Reverse the curse of the spirit of reasoning!

Satan came to destroy or disrupt three important things, the understanding of the Timing of the Holy Spirit and Revelation of the correct interpretation of his written word! Which is order of the Holy spirits written word! Satan went after Eve first the Choice Fat Marrow! He manifested himself into the bones! The red blood cells and process of healing and everything else is manufactured in the bones red bone marrow! He came to destroy the written order of his Word and Revelation of the correct understanding and disrupt the Timing! Unity is timing, order and intimacy of Character of Christ with the Holy Spirit! He went after order, which is the disruption of marriage, marriage he went after their unity to be one, and the hidden mystery was to disrupt spiritual timing!

Three mechanisms order, spiritual timing and Unity! Father Order, Unity Christ son, Holy Spirit spiritual timing and order! Holy Spirit is the mystery! There're so many divorces in marriage, so much division in the body of Christ, which is the church! Ignorance gets us in trouble! We do not have the correct understanding of his word, we do not take heed to his instructions, and our disobedience is based out of our reasoning! We reason when it comes to emptying ourselves, dying to self or dying to self-will! You make your own self believe what you're talking about! Self-denial and Denial!

Chapter 6

Paul the apostle went to the forest for three years to be taught by the Holy Spirit! Now a certain Jew named Apollos, born at Alexandria, an eloquent man and mighty in Scriptures, came to Ephesus. This man had been instructed in the way of the Lord, and being fervent in spirit, he spoke and taught accurately the things of the Lord, though he knew only the baptism of John. So he began to speak boldly in the synagogue.
When Aquila and Priscilla heard him, they took him aside and explained to him the way of God more accurately (Acts 18:24-26). There is Order of the Holy Spirit, Timing of the Holy spirit and there Order of the written word of the Holy Spirit! The letter kills but the spirit gives life to the word! Paul once stated I can knock each and every one of you out by the spirit and power of God but didn't!

Let us move on Saints, more clarification, **2 Corinthians 12:7, or because of these surpassingly great revelations. Therefore, in order to keep me from becoming conceited, I was given a thorn in my flesh, a messenger of Satan, to torment me.**

Now let us recap what thorn in his flesh was by Revelation of the Holy Spirit. Paul the Apostle was burdened by something or was in a suffering stage with the Holy Spirit. We all know the Holy Spirit can be grieved.

Joshua 23:13 "Know for a certainty that the Lord your God will no more drive out any of these nations from before you; but they shall be snares and traps unto you, and scourges in your sides, and thorns in your eyes, until ye perish from off this good land which the LORD your God hath given you."

Numbers 33:55 "But if ye will not drive out the inhabitants of the land from before you; then it shall come to pass, that those which ye let remain of them shall be pricks in your eyes, and thorns in your sides, and shall vex you in the land wherein ye dwell."

Ok thorn in your side means a vexation against you or discouragement or tormenting figure of some sort or burdened or a type of bondage. This is the Burden that was needed to carry, ever since the beginning of time In the Garden This disruption was impregnated by Satan into Eve. Let us continue, what was the burden that Paul was carrying was, he was feeling the disruption of the Apostolic Kingdom and the suffering of the Ministry of God's Chosen people walking out of the timing, Order and Will of the Holy Spirit!

When your given such Great Revelation, Gods children and his Apostolic ministry usually is not ready for it or can understand it due to lack of Timing, order and will of the Holy spirit individually for themselves! Watch this, **Acts 16: 6 Now when they had gone throughout Phrygia and the region of Galatia, and were forbidden of the Holy Ghost to preach the word in Asia. They were forbidden to speak and teach and Minister his word!** This is considered unforbidden Knowledge, unforbidden access etc. This Revelation is also in my 6th book.

1 Corinthians 15:8 and last of all he was seen of me also, as of one born out of due time. Paul the Apostle was taught by the Holy spirit in the wilderness 3years and felt saw the Apostolic movement the kingdom and the future of our Apostolic Ministry Today out of Alignment! He carried the Burden when he was living and suffered from it due to the Great Testimony of Revelation of Knowing the Holy Spirit and Yahushua, Christ

Himself!

You notice his side the rib, where it all started from the Beginning in the Garden Adam and Eve! The bone marrow was interrupted and disrupted! Then you notice Christ himself became the completed work and was Pierced in his side on the cross (The Rib) for the Redemption, Rebirth and Resurrection Testimony of it to be Completed and Unleashed and Released back into Alignment!

Let us go to **Philippians 3: 7 But whatever were gains to me I now consider loss for the sake of Christ. 8 What is more, I consider everything a loss because of the surpassing worth of knowing Christ Jesus my Lord, for whose sake I have lost all things. I consider them garbage, that I may gain Christ 9 and be found in him, not having a righteousness of my own that comes from the law, but that which is through faith in[a] Christ—the righteousness that comes from God on the basis of faith. 10 I want to know Christ—yes, to know the power of his resurrection and participation in his sufferings, becoming like him in his death, 11 and so, somehow, attaining to the resurrection from the dead.**

12 Not that I have already obtained all this, or have already arrived at my goal, but I press on to take hold of that for which Christ Jesus took hold of me. (Until Christ himself takes hold of us completely) 13 Brothers and sisters, I do not consider myself yet to have taken hold of it. But one thing I do: Forgetting what is behind and straining toward what is ahead, 14 I press on toward the goal to win the prize for which God has called me heavenward in Christ Jesus

15 All of us, then, who are mature should take such a view of things. And if on some point you think differently, that too

God will make clear to you. 16 Only let us live up to what we have already attained.

Now some of you are taught to name it and claim it scenarios, You have already attained it now let the work of The Holy spirit, the timing, the leading, the will and order of it take full dominion over you and possess you! You need to die to self, self-will and Die to the desire of wanting to succeed and prosper until Christ himself becomes all in all in you!

Can I get a wat wat, woo woo, just being funny. Now 5/1/2016 My spiritual mother and also Biological received a revelation from Holy spirit to read Psalms 18.This was a right now word that was given to Her to Release and I also over heard the conversation and looked into the matter with depth and searched out the scriptures in Hebrew and by the Holy spirit for more Revelation of what the right now word what saying by Holy spirit was speaking of. I was awakened at 3am in the morning.

Psalms 18:29 With your help I can advance against a troop ,with my God I can (scale) a (wall).Look attentively at scale and wall. Troop in Hebrew means From Gadad; a crowd (especially of soldiers) -- army, band (of men), company, troop (of robbers). Genesis 49:19 "As for [f]Gad—a raiding troop shall raid him, But he shall raid at their heels _and_ assault them [victoriously].

Scale in Hebrew Is Mozen, it states its just a pair of scales. We all know scales are used for weighing, silver and gold. I also looked up the word wall in Hebrew, its Chamah to Create, to build to Enjoy safety. **Deuteronomy 8:18 But remember the LORD your God, for it is he who gives you the ability to produce wealth, and so confirms his covenant, which he swore**

to your ancestors, as it is today. Scale or leaping over a wall is to produce, to prosper overcome and achieve any obstacle by his right hand Yahweh.

Then Holy Spirit directed me to **Proverbs 18:11 The wealth of the rich is their fortified city; they imagine it a wall too high to scale.** There fortress is their riches and think they cannot be overcome. **Provers 21:22 A wise man scales the city walls of the mighty and brings down the stronghold in which they trust. We all know that the wealth of the rich is their Heart, and there silver and Gold the fortress or fortified city, their wealth.**

Then he directed me to **Amos 1:7 [7] But I will send a fire on the (wall of Gaza), which shall devour the palaces thereof.** So I asked the Holy spirit where are you going with all of this, but was so excited about it too. Then he said go to **Acts 8: [26] But an angel of the Lord said to Philip, Rise and proceed southward *or* at midday on the road that runs from (Jerusalem down to Gaza). This is the desert [[g]route].**

[27] So he got up and went. And behold, an Ethiopian, a eunuch of great authority under Candace the queen of the Ethiopians, who was in charge of all her treasure, had come to Jerusalem to worship. This official was in charge of the all her treasure the wealth, the Queen of Ethiopians.

(Did you get the Revelation I am sending, speaking, Manifested, Transitioning, Giving you all your resources, needs, Hearts desires, promises, wealth, Prosperity, empty desolate places, lost hope, resurrecting everything in your life now today!)

[34] And the eunuch said to Philip, I beg of you, tell me about whom does the prophet say this, about himself or about

someone else?

³⁵ Then Philip opened his mouth, and beginning with this portion of Scripture he announced to him the glad tidings (Gospel) of Jesus *and* about Him. ³⁶ And as they continued along on the way, they came to some water, and the eunuch exclaimed, See, [here is] water! What is to hinder my being baptized? ³⁷ [k]*And Philip said, If you believe with all your heart [if you have* [l]*a conviction, full of joyful trust, that Jesus is the Messiah and accept Him as the Author of your salvation in the kingdom of God, giving Him your obedience, then] you may. And he replied, I do believe that Jesus Christ is the Son of God.*

³⁸ And he ordered that the chariot be stopped; and both Philip and the eunuch went down into the water, and [Philip] baptized him.

You notice the father sets fire also on the hearts of men to bring them to Salvation, and also he sets fire on their fortresses the wealth, only fire can Transfer to Liquid state. He has transferred the Wealth, riches and resources of promise into our hands!

Setting fire on the silver and gold to Liquidate to us, transferring it over. I am resurrection your dry places in every need, your heart and needs, your desires and needs of promise!

Continuing **Psalms 18: ³³ He makes my feet like hinds' feet [able to stand firmly or make progress on the dangerous heights of testing and trouble]; He sets me securely upon my high places. Then he said go to Habakkuk 3:19 The Lord God is my strength. He will set my feet like the deer. He will let me walk upon the heights.**

Heights is also a place of Responsibility!!! Deer's leap and dwell on hills and mountains. **Psalms 50:10 for every animal of the forest is mine, and the cattle on a thousand hills.**

Cattle carried the Ark of the Covenant the glory of God and also, they carried silver and gold in the Old Testament!

PROPHET ANTHONY MONTOYA

About Prophet Anthony Montoya

From a divorced, homeless and hopeless situation, The Lord has anointed Anthony Montoya and he is mightily being used of The Holy Spirit with an insightful prophetic word designed for you to experience Yahshua's presence and power, break the bonds of demonic influence, deal with stress and give you victory through Yahshua.

Since I'm an ordained minister, my belief is to be a life living sacrifice for Yahweh's kingdom, only to be servant to others and help one another reach Yahweh's purpose and destiny in our lives.

It is to unveil the mysteries and revelations of this kingdom age for all his children to be set free from religion, jezebel spirits, spirit of influence, psychology, false hope (false prophesies), rejection, abandonment guilt, shame, control, seared conscious, subconscious, conscious, mesocratic cells , trauma, familiar spirits, camellia spirits that transforms and changes color, cockatrice spirit, the false god of Prosperity, Fortune & Destiny, mystical influences that general spirits have had dominion over us.

Made in the USA
Las Vegas, NV
26 March 2022

46344842R00028